EX LIBRIS

WILLIAM SLOAN UPTON

Idylls of France

IDYLLS ⚜OF FRANCE

Photographed and Edited by PROCTOR JONES

Foreword by IRVING STONE

DEDICATION

To my lusty French ancestors,
early settlers of Detroit and Montreal,
and to my mentor in this work,
James P. Barry, Esq., scholar, writer, artist, and friend

Giverny

Contents

Foreword

This book is a love affair between Proctor Jones, one of America's most sensitive photographers, and the immortal beauty of the French landscape. As with all good love affairs, the reader emerges with a sense of awe and fulfillment. The beauty of the book can be shared with friends, and bring about happy reminiscences.

Proctor Jones had a delightful idea, some twenty years ago: to find the best writings about the French countryside, and then search out, with his variety of cameras, those scenes either described by the authors or best illuminating their poetic-prose passages. And so, along with the breath-taking pictures, we read a number of the finest passages from Robert Louis Stevenson, Henry James, Mark Twain, Henry Adams, Edith Wharton, H. A. Taine; great writers, all.

In a world which daily grows more crazy and unlivable, it is heartening to have this book at hand. Proctor Jones spent years traveling over the physical face of France, and over the typeface of authors who journeyed through France, and loved what they saw. As a result, with *Idylls of France* we can go back in time, see the loveliness of the earth as it was created and remolded by Man; and read the refreshing passages written by some of our most articulate minds.

I have my own favorite photographs and literary passages in this book; but I would not attempt to impose them on the reader. Each of you will find your own special views and reflections; and probably return to them many times.

Of most recommended books we can say, "Have a good read." With *Idylls of France* we say, "Have a good view *and* a good read."

Irving Stone

Beverly Hills
May, 1982

Afternoon at Le Bec

About the Authors

The travels of Arthur Young and Thomas Jefferson covered approximately the same period. Jefferson travelled widely in France during the time he was American Envoy, following the American Revolution. Arthur Young, an established English agronomist, arrived in France in 1787 to study and report on French agriculture. He found himself swept up in events which led to the French Revolution. His connection with members of the royal household caused him considerable trouble. However, his studies were found to be important by the revolutionary government, which succeeded Louis XVI. They were translated, reproduced, and widely-circulated.

The early nineteenth century finds Henry Wadsworth Longfellow, James Fenimore Cooper, and Thomas Adolphus Trollope writing of their experiences in France. Longfellow was a very young man when he wrote *Outre-Mer*. During this trip he became an authority on the songs of the trouveres, the troubadours. Trollope developed a great deal of material on Brittany and the early mystery plays. He travelled mainly on foot. With his brother Anthony and their mother, he at one time lived in the United States.

James Fenimore Cooper came to France with his family in 1826, and remained abroad for more than six years. His stories are enlivened with interesting eyewitness accounts. For example, he met Sir Walter Scott in Paris, and was a friend of General Lafayette.

"Aguecheek," whose voyage to France must have predated the American Civil War, preferred to remain anonymous. Anyone desiring to study the suggested preparations for a European tour at that time will find his work entertaining.

Toward the end of the century, excellent writing about France was accomplished by John Ruskin, Henry James, Henry Adams, Mark Twain, S. Baring-Gould, Robert Louis Stevenson, Walter Pater and James Russell Lowell. Ruskin, who is respected as a great art and architectural authority, made many trips to France, starting as a young boy travelling with his father. James, an acclaimed literary lion, made a relaxed trip through France, writing easily and with understanding of what he saw. Henry Adams wrote about Mont-Saint-Michel and Chartres for his friends. The work has become definitive on the subject.

Mark Twain made several European trips. *The Innocents Abroad* was written about his experiences during his first tour. In later years he returned, and living in France wrote, among other works, a serious study of Joan of Arc.

Baring-Gould is not broadly-read today. He was a prolific writer on many subjects including travel studies. A graduate of Cambridge University, he became a minister. At one point, he wrote the words to "Onward Christian Soldiers" and "Now the Day is Over." He probed deeply into the

City Hall at Marseilles

French countryside and amassed much interesting, detailed information which he generously passes along to the reader.

Stevenson made two interesting trips into France in the 1870's. His travel plan included more than just a casual pleasure trip. He put himself into situations which were exciting. His canoe trip down the Oise, and his pack-trip with Modestine in central France, brought him close to the earth, which he understood and appreciated. Walter Pater, a pre-Raphaelite essayist and critic, wrote detailed essays upon the Renaissance masters. *Gaston De Latour* was published after his death in 1894.

Lines have been taken from James Russell Lowell's "The Cathedral." Not only a great poet and critic, he was also an accomplished diplomat, serving as Ambassador in Spain and England. He was the first editor of the *Atlantic Monthly.* It was his grandfather, a member of the Constitutional Convention, who coined the expression, "All men are created free and equal."

Two great French writers, much-translated into English, provide some native recognition of their country's beauty. Alphonse Daudet, who has been a guest of every French class in the United States, tells the story of his mill. Professor H. A. Taine, historian, scholar, and teacher, had reason to cover France thoroughly, as he was the Director of Public Instruction. His many official visits throughout the country provided him with an ample and interesting fund of material.

Edith Wharton not only travelled through France, she lived there. She came to a deep understanding of, and respect for, the French people, and she rejoiced in the richness of the country.

The great artist Claude Monet, father of Impressionism, wrote the message of his corner of France in his paintings of the Norman countryside and his water lily pond at Giverny, where he came to live in 1883.

Abbey Church, Le Bec Hellouin

Introduction

FRANCE!

Why, with all the other land in the world, is France the place?

Since the time that travellers found direction, paths have led to the valley of the Loire, the island of Lutèce, the orchards of Picardy, the meadows of Normandy, the mysteries of Brittany, the wildness of the Bocage, the heights of the Pyrenees, the soft and sunny coast of the Côte d'Or, the mountain fastness of the Alps, the Jura, the Vosges, and the Cevennes.

Since Julius Caesar, the travel record has been kept: "All Gaul is divided in three parts. . . ." Here, the first taste of France. The appetite is whetted, even though the Latin lesson of the day is long forgotten.

Since then, men and women of letters have spent much time telling others of their exploits.

Some criticized, some made fun, some longed for home, and some wrote masterpieces.

All marvelled at Nature's gifts to this unique land.

That the real estate of France is not lost on those from other stretches of the globe may be judged by the variety of groups passing through the Louvre each day (except Tuesday). Clutched firmly in the traveller's hand: a Guide Michelin, or a Guide Bleu, or a Guide something else; around the neck, or in the other hand, a camera. The combination cannot miss. It is difficult to find an unwilling photographic subject in France.

Included in our company will be some old travel hands—Henry Wadsworth Longfellow, Henry Adams, John Ruskin, Thomas Adolphus Trollope, Edith Wharton, Mark Twain, and Henry James, to name a few.

Warm and entertaining guides they are, though here and there a freeway, unforeseen by them, cuts across a piece of classic description.

These photographs are inspired by their invitation.

So, with the help of a shadow, a turning leaf, a raindrop, a soaring spire, this collection brings to you, quite simply, IDYLLS of FRANCE.

Proctor Jones

San Francisco
July 14, 1982

Normandy Roadway

For my part, I travel not to go anywhere, but to go.
I travel for travel's sake. The great affair is to move;
to feel the needs and hitches of our life more nearly;
to come down off this featherbed of civilization, and
find the globe granite underfoot and strewn with
cutting flints. Alas, as we get up in life, and are more
preoccupied with our affairs, even a holiday is a thing
that must be worked for. To hold a pack upon a pack-
saddle against a gale out of the freezing north is no
high industry, but it is one that serves to occupy and
compose the mind. And when the present is so exact-
ing, who can annoy himself about the future?

ROBERT LOUIS STEVENSON, *Travels with a Donkey in the Cevennes*, 1879

Coast of Brittany

The Pays d'Outre-Mer, or the Land beyond the Sea,
is a name by which the pilgrims and crusaders of old
usually designated the Holy Land. I, too, in a certain
sense, have been a pilgrim of Outre-Mer; for to my
youthful imagination the Old World was a kind of
Holy Land, lying afar off beyond the blue horizon of
the ocean; and when its shores first rose upon my
sight, looming through the hazy atmosphere of the
sea, my heart swelled with the deep emotions of the
pilgrim when he sees afar the spire which rises above
the shrine of his devotion.

HENRY WADSWORTH LONGFELLOW, *Outre-Mer*, 1833

Transept, Rouen Cathedral

Arches above arches, supported by a forest of massive
columns, seemed to be climbing up as if they aspired
to reach the throne. The sun was obscured by a passing
cloud as I entered, and that made the ancient arches
seem doubly solemn. I walked halfway up the aisle,
and stopped on hearing voices at a distance. As I stood
listening, the sun uncovered his radiant face, and
poured his golden glory through the great western
windows of the church. At the same moment a clear
tenor voice rang out from the choir as if the sunbeams
had called it into being.

"AGUECHEEK," *My Unknown Chum*, c.1858

Ancient Street, Dinan

Wherever Christian church architecture has been good and lovely, it has been merely the perfect development of the common dwelling-house architecture of the period; when the pointed arch was used in the street, it was used in the church; when the round arch was used in the street, it was used in the church; when the pinnacle was set over the garret window, it was set over the belfry tower; when the flat roof was used for the drawing-room, it was used for the nave. There is no sacredness in round arches, nor in pointed; none in pinnacles, nor in buttresses; none in pillars, nor in traceries. Churches were never built in any separate, mystical, and religious style; they were built in the manner that was common and familiar to everybody at the time.

JOHN RUSKIN, *Stones of Venice*, 1853

Avranches

The extent of country, which the eye looks over from the gardens and terraces of Avranches is extremely pretty. Nor is the town itself void of objects of curiosity and interest. But the cathedral is no more. The ruins of it even have almost entirely disappeared.

It was in front of this church that Henry II of England met the pope's legates to answer before them the charge of Becket's murder.

In the twelfth century, Avranches was celebrated for its trouveres. The little court, which Henry, the younger son of the Conqueror, held at Avranches, was principally composed of a knot of poets. It is said, too, that at Avranches, first were acted those scriptural dramas, which under the name of mysteries became so favourite a pastime in the earlier part of the middle ages.

THOMAS ADOLPHUS TROLLOPE, *A Summer in Western France*, 1841

Mont-Saint-Michel

Saint Michael held a place of his own in heaven and on earth which seems, in the eleventh century, to leave hardly room for the Virgin of the Crypt at Chartres, still less for the Beau Christ of the thirteenth century at Amiens. The Archangel stands for Church and State, and both militant. His place was where the danger was greatest; therefore you find him here. For the same reason he was, while the pagan danger lasted, the patron saint of France. So the Normans, when they were converted to Christianity, put themselves under his powerful protection. He stood for centuries on his Mount in Peril of the Sea. So soldiers, nobles, and monarchs went on pilgrimage to his shrine; so the common people followed, and still follow, like ourselves.

HENRY ADAMS, *Mont-Saint-Michel and Chartres,* 1905

Sand, Tide, Shadow, Mont-Saint-Michel

The church at Mont-Saint-Michel stands high on the summit of this granite rock, and on its west front is the platform, to which the tourist ought first to climb. From the edge of this platform, the eye plunges down, two hundred and thirty-five feet, to the wide sands or the wider ocean, as the tides recede or advance, under an infinite sky.

HENRY ADAMS, *Mont-Saint-Michel and Chartres*, 1905

26

The Marvel, Mont-Saint-Michel

A conscientious student has yet to climb down the many steps, on the outside, and look up at the Merveille from below. Few buildings in France are better worth the trouble. Taking architecture as an expression of energy, you should first note that here, in the eleventh century, the Church, however simple-minded or unschooled, was not cheap. Its self-respect is worth noticing, because it was short-lived in its art. Mont-Saint-Michel, throughout, even up to the delicate and intricate stonework of its cloisters, is built of granite. The crypts and substructures are as well constructed as the surfaces most exposed to view. When we get to Chartres, which is largely twelfth-century work, you will see that the cathedral there, too, is superbly built, of the hardest and heaviest stone within reach, which has nowhere settled or given way. The thirteenth century did not build so. The great cathedrals after 1200 show economy, and sometimes worse.

HENRY ADAMS, *Mont-Saint-Michel and Chartres*, 1905

Country Road at Morières

I wish our way had always lain among woods. Trees are the most vital society. An old oak that has been growing where he stands since before the Reformation, taller than many spires, more stately than the greater part of mountains, and yet a living thing, liable to sicknesses and death like you and me: is not that in itself a speaking lesson in history?

ROBERT LOUIS STEVENSON, *An Inland Voyage*, 1879

The Ancient Bishops of Chartres

It rose before me, patiently remote
From the great tides of life it breasted once,
Hearing the noise of men as in a dream.
I stood before the triple port,
Where dedicated shapes of saints and kings,
Stern faces bleared with immemorial watch,
Looked down benignly grave and seemed to say,
"Ye come and go incessant; we remain
Safe in the hallowed quiets of the past;
Be reverent, ye who flit and are forgot,
Of faith so nobly realized as this . . ."

JAMES RUSSELL LOWELL, *The Cathedral*, 1870

Mont Blanc, Chamonix

The fog hangs in the distance like soaked tiles, the near ones float in the evening like motionless gauze. The constantly-watered grass looks as if it would never wither. Here and there is a sleepy river, with long bright sheets of water, quiet and almost black, like the surface of a marsh, which reflects the sky as in a mirror. Even the face and form of humanity has changed; the people are taller, less lively, less cheerful and familiar. The universal greenness and moisture, the firs and the mountains, breed a sadder and more serious idea of life. One shudders slightly at the thought of winter, prepares oneself against it, and adds to the comforts of one's house.

H. A. TAINE, *Journeys Through France*, 1865

The Cathedral, Strasbourg

How well the men of old understood the effect of
light and shade! This Cathedral of Strasbourg speaks
to the eyes at once, and in its entirety. Words cannot
paint this vast avenue of stone, with its solemn pillars
in regular courses, never weary under the burden of
that sublime vault.

H. A. TAINE, *Journeys Through France*, 1865

The Valley of the Dordogne

We have come five hundred miles by rail through the heart of France. What a bewitching land it is! What a garden! Surely the leagues of bright green lawns are swept and brushed and watered every day and their grasses trimmed by the barber. Surely the hedges are shaped and measured and their symmetry preserved by the most architectural of gardeners. Surely the long, straight rows of stately poplars that divide the beautiful landscape like the squares of a checker-board are set with line and plummet, and their uniform height determined with a spirit level. Surely the straight, smooth, pure white turnpikes are jack-planed and sand-papered every day. How else are these marvels of symmetry, cleanliness, and order attained? It is wonderful. There are no unsightly stone walls, and never a fence of any kind. There is no dirt, no decay, no rubbish anywhere—nothing that even hints at untidiness—nothing that ever suggests neglect. All is orderly and beautiful—everything is charming to the eye.

MARK TWAIN, *The Innocents Abroad*, 1870

A Resting Place, near Amiens

Marriage, in France, is regarded as founded for the family and not for the husband and wife. It is designed not to make two people individually happy for a longer or shorter time, but to secure their permanent well-being as associates in the foundation of a home and the procreation of a family. Such an arrangement must needs be based on what is most permanent in human states of feeling, and least dependent on the accidents of beauty, youth, and novelty. Community of tradition, of education, and, above all, of the parental feeling, are judged to be the sentiments most likely to form a lasting tie between the average man and woman; and the French marriage is built upon parenthood, not on passion.

EDITH WHARTON, *French Ways and Their Meaning*, 1918

In the Countryside near Foix

There are several ways in which the Frenchwoman's relations with men may be called more important than those of her American sister. In the first place, in the commercial class, the Frenchwoman is always her husband's business partner. The lives of the French bourgeois couple are based on the primary necessity of getting enough money to live on, and of giving their children educational and material advantages. In small businesses the woman is always her husband's book-keeper or clerk, or both; above all, she is his business advisor.

EDITH WHARTON, *French Ways and Their Meaning*, 1918

Marseilles, Place Castellane

Marseilles is monumental and grandiose; its life is
fuller and more spacious than that of Paris. It is the
most prosperous and magnificent of Latin cities.
Nothing like it has been seen on the Mediterranean
shores since the most famous days of Alexandria,
Rome, or Carthage.

H. A. TAINE, *Journeys Through France*, 1865

A Norman Countryside

On every side, valley and hill were covered with a carpet of soft velvet green. Here and there a cluster of chestnut-trees shaded a cottage, and little patches of vineyard were scattered on the slope of the hills, mingling their delicate green with the deep hues of the early summer grain. The whole landscape had a fresh, breezy look. It was not hedged in from the highways but lay open to the eye of the traveller, and seemed to welcome him with open arms. I felt less a stranger in the land; and as my eye traced the dusty road winding along through a rich cultivated country, skirted on either side with blossoming fruit-trees, and occasionally caught glimpses of a little farm-house resting in a green hollow and lapped in the bosom of plenty, I felt that I was in a prosperous, hospitable, and happy land.

HENRY WADSWORTH LONGFELLOW, *Outre-Mer*, 1833

Rouen, The Great Clock

I had seen so many old cities that I had no thought of
getting enthusiastic about Rouen, until I found myself
suddenly in a state of mental exaltation. I had visited
Rouen as many people visit churches and galleries
of art in Italy —because I had the opportunity, and
feared that in after years I might be asked if I had ever
been there. But, if a dislike to acknowledge my
ignorance led me to Rouen, it was a very different
sentiment that took possession of me as soon as I
caught the spirit of the place. The genius of the past
seemed to inhabit every street and alley of that strange
city. Rouen was, of all the cities of France, the richest
in those objects with which the painter's mind had
the profoundest sympathy. All was at unity with
itself, and the city lay, under its guarding hills, one
labyrinth of delight, its grey and fretted towers, misty
in their magnificence of height, letting the sky like
blue enamel through the foiled spaces of their crowns
of open work; the walls and gates, of its countless
churches wardered by saintly groups of solemn statuary.

"AGUECHEEK," *My Unknown Chum,* c.1858

The Pont du Gard

You are very near the Pont du Gard before you see it; the ravine it spans suddenly opens and exhibits the picture. Over the valley, from side to side, and ever so high in the air, stretch the three tiers of the tremendous bridge. They are unspeakably imposing. The hugeness, the solidity, the unexpectedness, the monumental rectitude of the whole thing leave you nothing to say. The number of arches in each tier is different; they are smaller and more numerous as they ascend. The preservation of the thing is extraordinary; nothing has crumbled or collapsed; every feature remains, and the huge blocks of stone, of a brownish-yellow (as if they had been baked by the Provençal sun for eighteen centuries), pile themselves, without mortar or cement, as evenly as the day they were laid together. All this to carry the water of a couple of springs to a little provincial city!

HENRY JAMES, *A Little Tour In France,* 1884

The Loire near Ancenis

Between Angers and Nantes, the Loire is probably one
of the finest rivers in the world, the breadth of the
stream, the islands of woods, the boldness, culture,
and richness of the coast, all conspire, with the ani-
mation derived from the swelling canvass of active
commerce, to render that line eminently beautiful.

ARTHUR YOUNG, *Travels in France*, 1787-89

Kerduel and King Arthur

We turned off to visit the chateau of Kerduel, which is situated in the parish of Pleumeur-Bodou. Lovers of early romance will hardly think that labour lost which places them on a spot so celebrated in the chronicles of the period as the favourite residence of King Arthur. Here places and names surround us, with which the romance of the round table have made us familiar, but to which Fancy has assigned a locality in fairy-land rather than in any veritable portion of the earth's surface. Here the half-fictitious personages, whose adventures have in so many forms amused us, and the mystic performers of those deeds, which have bequeathed to Europe an heroical literature of her own, have "a local habitation and a name." Here it was that Arthur held his brilliant court.

THOMAS ADOLPHUS TROLLOPE, *A Summer in Brittany*, 1840

The Great River Residence of Francis I at Blois

The Chateau de Blois is one of the most beautiful and elaborate of all the old royal residences. As you cross its threshold you step straight into the sunshine and storm of the French Renaissance. On your right is the wing erected by Francis I. This exquisite, this extravagant, this transcendent piece of architecture is the most joyous utterance of the French Renaissance. It is covered with embroidery of sculpture in which every detail is worthy of the hand of a goldsmith. Every inch of this structure, of its balconies, its pillars, its great central columns, is wrought over with lovely images, strange and ingenious devices, prime among which is the great heraldic salamander of Francis I.

HENRY JAMES, *A Little Tour In France,* 1884

From the Tower of the Cathedral of Orleans

The view from the top tower of the cathedral church
is a wide one, for Orleans stands in the centre of the
largest plain in France. Some remnants of the ancient
forest of Orleans might be described to the eastward,
and to the westward the eye could trace the course of
the river for many a league, here losing it as it wound
under some vine covered bank a little higher than the
general elevation of the flat plain through which it
meanders, and there again recognizing it by the
sparkle and play of the morning sun upon some elbow
of the stream when it swelled into a wider expanse
of water.

THOMAS ADOLPHUS TROLLOPE, *A Summer in Western France*, 1841

Chateau of Chambord on the Loire

Frequently, along the great historic Stream, as along some vast street, contemporary genius was visible in a novel and seductive architecture, which, by its engrafting of exotic grace on homely native forms, spoke of a certain restless aspiration to be what one was not but might become—the old Gaulish desire to be refined, to be mentally enfranchised by the sprightlier genius of Italy. With their terraced gardens, their airy galleries, their triumphal chimney-pieces, their spacious stairways, their conscious provision for the elegant enjoyment of all seasons in turn, here surely were the new abodes for the new humanity of this new, poetic, picturesque age.

WALTER PATER, *Gaston De Latour*, 1896

Mountains South of Grenoble on the Route Napoleon

To what cause it is owing I cannot tell, nor is it generally allowed or felt; but of the fact I am certain, that for grace of stem and perfection of form in their transparent foliage, the French trees are altogether unmatched; and their modes of grouping and massing are so perfectly and constantly beautiful that I think of all countries for educating the artist to the perception of grace, France bears the bell, of which there is not a single valley but is full of the most lovely pictures, nor a mile from which the artist may not receive instruction.

JOHN RUSKIN, *Modern Painters*, 1846

A River Landing near Taillebourg

We must all set our pocket watches by the clock of fate. There is a headlong, forthright tide, that bears away man with his fancies like a straw, and runs fast in time and space. The river is full of curves like this, and lingers and returns in pleasant pastorals; and yet, rightly thought upon, never returns at all. For though it should revisit the same acre of meadow in the same hour, it will have made an ample sweep between-whiles; many little streams will have fallen in; many exhalations risen towards the sun; and even although it were the same acre it will not more be the same river.

ROBERT LOUIS STEVENSON, *An Inland Voyage*, 1879

The Battlefield at Crécy

We passed through, or near, the field of Cressy. By the aid of the books, we fancied we could trace the positions of the two armies, but it was little more than very vague conjecture. There was a mead, a breadth of field well adapted to cavalry, and a wood. The river is a mere brook, and could have offered but little protection, or resistance, to the passage of any species of troops. I saw no village.

We have anglicized the word Cressy, which the French term Crecy, or, to give it a true Picard orthography, Creci. The French very ingeniously assert that the English armies of old were principally composed of Norman soldiers, and that the chivalrous nobility which performed such wonders were of purely Norman blood.

JAMES FENIMORE COOPER, *Gleanings in Europe (France)*, 1836

The Harbor at La Rochelle

I followed a shady walk which forms part of the old rampart of La Rochelle. It is very charming, winding and wandering, always with trees. Beneath the rampart is a tidal river, and on the other side, for a long distance, the mossy walls of the immense garden of a seminary. Tour de l'Horloge separates the town proper from the port; for beyond the old gray arch the place presents its bright, expressive little face to the sea.

HENRY JAMES, *A Little Tour In France,* 1884

Looking to the Western Pyrenees

The whole region of the Pyrenees is of a nature and aspect so totally different from everything I had been accustomed to, that these excursions were productive of much amusement. Cultivation is here carried to a considerable perfection in several articles, especially in the irrigation of meadows: we seek out the most intelligent farmers and have many and long conversations with those who understand French, which however is not the case with all, for the language of the country is a mixture of Catalan, Provençal, and French.

ARTHUR YOUNG, *Travels in France, 1787-89*

The Pyrenees, A Basque Shepherd

The Basques are a people of great interest to the
ethnologist, as the last shrunken remains of that
Iberian race that once occupied all Western Europe
from Scotland to Portugal and Spain, and, indeed,
overleaped the Straits and spread as Kabyles and
Berbers in Northern Africa. Although overlapped
by other races, this Basque element forms the main
constituent of the French race in the south-west.

S. BARING-GOULD, *A Book of the Pyrenees,* 1907

On the Path of Charlemagne and Roland, St. Jean Pied du Port

I cannot convey an adequate idea of the beauty, the calm, the delightful softness of the scene; that would need the pencil of a Decamps or a Corot. The clear sky shines out above like the pearly lining of a shell, the broad sheet of water reflects its light, and the upper and the under glow meet and float impalpably in the delicate breath of the mist. This transparent veil of air softens every outline; the slim trees seem to be turned to vapour. They might be happy shades floating between existence and extinction, softly, yearningly, as ready to vanish as to reappear.

H. A. TAINE, *Journeys Through France*, 1865

Springs of La Raillere

At Cauterets the spring of La Raillere is at some
distance from the town. It takes its name from the
avalanches (railleres) that have made their pathway
down the mountain side above it, and have left their
white and ghastly scars on the rocks, and heaped
wreckage below. This is the most abundant group of
springs, but the space there is narrow, and lies in a
gorge. The thermal establishment has to be main-
tained on huge walled terraces. Those who use the
waters for baths or for gargling come and go by the
tram. The platform on which the baths of La Raillere
are constituted command a view of the deep valley of
Lutour, down which descends a stream issuing from a
chain of little lakes lying in the lap of the Pic de
Mallerouge.

S. BARING-GOULD, *A Book of the Pyrenees*, 1907

Giverny, Monet's Lily Pond

The water lilies of my pond at Giverny are my
life . . . you find here all the motifs that I have used
from 1905-1914. I have painted a great deal of the
water lilies, modifying my angle of view each time.
The motifs change according to the seasons of the year
and with the differences of the ever-changing light.
The effect changes constantly not only from season to
season but from one minute to the next. But these
water flowers are far from being the whole picture. To
speak the truth, they are only the accompaniment.
The essential motif is the water's mirror reflecting the
constantly-changing sky; the passing clouds and the
breeze. To catch this perpetual change it is necessary
to work with five or six canvases at the same time.

CLAUDE MONET, *La Revue de l'Art,* 1927 (Thiébault-Sisson)

The Gorge of the Tarn

A new road leads from the Pont de Montvert to
Florac by the valley of the Tarn; a smooth sandy ledge,
it runs about half-way between the summit of the
cliffs and the river in the bottom of the valley. This
was a pass like that of Killiecrankie; a deep turning
gully in the hills, with the Tarn making a wonderful
hoarse uproar far below.

ROBERT LOUIS STEVENSON, *Travels with a Donkey in the Cevennes,* 1879

Pradelles, High in the Cevennes with Snow in May

Pradelles stands on a hillside, high above the Allier, surrounded by rich meadows. Over this the clouds shed a uniform and purplish shadow, sad and somewhat menacing, exaggerating height and distance.

ROBERT LOUIS STEVENSON, *Travels with a Donkey in the Cevennes*, 1879

St. Jean du Gard, South of the Cevennes

I have not often enjoyed a place more deeply. I moved in an atmosphere of pleasure, and felt light and quiet and content. But perhaps it was not the place alone that so disposed my spirit. Perhaps someone was thinking of me in another country; or perhaps some thought of my own had come and gone unnoticed, and yet done me good. For some thoughts, which sure would be the most beautiful, vanish before we can rightly scan their features; as though a god, travelling by our green highways, should but ope the door, give one smiling look into the house, and go again for ever. Was it Apollo, or Mercury, or Love with folded wings? Who shall say? But we go the lighter about our business, and feel peace and pleasure in our hearts.

ROBERT LOUIS STEVENSON, *Travels with a Donkey in the Cevennes*, 1879

The Loire at Coubon

The river widens out towards the bridge, and glistens
like a sheet of ice under the placid sun. Straight in
front of me, on the wide, green, level plain, the light
foliage quivers, and the poplars rustle their few re-
maining leaves. The sky is flushed with brightness;
the air is flecked with diamonds between the slender
branches; the verdure clothes itself in softer tints, for,
though nourished by the stream, the sun has touched
it into brown or gold. The eyes are at rest amid this
deeper colouring; there comes a sense of joy as they
sweep the radiant surface of the water, and life once
more seems gracious and kind.

H. A. TAINE, *Journeys Through France*, 1865

Secret at Le Puy

At Le Puy, the plan of the church, S. Michel l'Aiguilhe, on the pinnacle of rock is peculiar, resembling the attitude of a sleeping dog. How did the builders of those days construct churches and donjons on the tops of these obelisks? Masons had to fill in all the rifts of the rock so as to form a terrace on which to build. They must have been let down in cradles. As to the tower, it was probably built up from within, as is done nowadays with a factory chimney. On a lower level than the doorway are the ruins of the habitation of the chaplain who served the church. He could obtain plenty of fresh air there to fill his lungs, but could not get exercise to circulate his blood, save by running up and down the stair in the face of the rock.

S. BARING-GOULD, *A Book of the Cevennes,* 1907

Remnant of a Noble Fortress near Le Puy

The Polignacs lent lustre to Le Velay. These masters
of the rock were brave nobles. They fought in the
Crusades; they fought the English. They espoused the
faith, the passions, the fervour of their native land.
As the feudal towers of Polignac dominated, and
dominate still, the green and flowery land that lies
spread below it, so does the name of Polignac dominate the history of Velay.

S. BARING-GOULD, *A Book of the Cevennes*, 1907

Maison Carré, Nîmes

I viewed Maison Quarre last night; again this morning, and twice more in the day; it is beyond all comparison the most light, elegant, and pleasing building I ever beheld. Without any magnitude to render it imposing; without any extraordinary magnificence to surprise, it rivets attention. There is a magic harmony in the proportions that charms the eye. One can fix on no particular part of the pre-eminent beauty; it is one perfect whole of symmetry and grace.

ARTHUR YOUNG, *Travels in France*, 1787-89

Here I am, Madam, gazing whole hours at the Maison quarree, like a lover at his mistress. The stocking-weavers and silk spinners around it consider me as an hypochondriac Englishman, about to write with a pistol the last chapter of his history. This is the second time I have been in love since I left Pâris.

THOMAS JEFFERSON, *To Madame de Tesse, Nismes*. March 20, 1787.

Daudet's Mill, near Saint-Rémy-de-Provence

The mill was a ruin; a crumbling mass of stone, iron and old boards which had not turned in the wind for many years and which lay, with broken limbs, useless. Strange affinities exist between ourselves and inanimate things. From the first day that cast-off structure was dear to my heart; I loved it for its desolation, its road overgrown with weeds, and for its little worn platform sheltered from the wind. With the creaking of an old building shaken by the north wind, the flapping of its ragged wings like the rigging of a ship at sea, the mill stirred in my poor, restless, nomadic brain memories of journeys by sea, or landings at lighthouses and far-off islands; and the shivering swell all about completed the illusion.

ALPHONSE DAUDET, *Thirty Years In Paris*, 1899

The Grimaldi Stronghold

Les Baux was not only a city, but a state; not only a state, but an empire; and on the crest of its little mountain called itself sovereign of a territory. The lords of Les Baux, in a word, were great feudal proprietors; and there was a time during which the island of Sardinia, to say nothing of places nearer home, such as Arles and Marseilles, paid them homage. We wandered down narrow, precipitous streets, bordered by empty houses with gaping windows and absent doors, through which we had glimpses of sculptured chimney-pieces and fragments of stately arch and vault. Some of the houses are still inhabited; but most of them are open to the air and weather. Some of them have completely collapsed; others present to the street a front which enables one to judge Les Baux in the days of its importance.

HENRY JAMES, *A Little Tour In France,* 1884

The Roman Theatre at Arles

In Arles I wandered among the Roman remains of
the arena by light of a magnificent moon. The effect
was admirable. As we sat in the theatre looking at the
two lone columns that survive —part of the decoration
of the back of the stage —and at the fragments of ruin
around them, we might have been in the Roman
Forum. The two slim columns stood there like a pair
of silent actors. The spot is one of the sweetest legacies
of the ancient world.

HENRY JAMES, *A Little Tour In France,* 1884

Base Rock of the Alps, near Marseilles

Near Marseilles, the structure of the rock might be fragments of marble kneaded together under some enormous pressure. It is stratified in courses, like stages of half-ruined towers. Some are sloped, and remind one of the remains of marble palaces built by Roman Emperors or Babylonian Kings. The divergent lines, the innumerable fractures, the infinitely diverse angles of the slopes, catch the light, and relieve the bareness of the great white walls with fantastic arabesques. All is full of life; the whole chain of the mountains is peopled with form and colour.

H. A. TAINE, *Journeys Through France*, 1865

The Prison of the Count of Monte Cristo

We hired a sailboat and a guide and made an excursion to one of the small islands in the harbor of Marseilles to visit the Castle d'If. This ancient fortress has a melancholy history. It has been used as a prison for political offenders for two or three hundred years, and its dungeon walls are scarred with the rudely carved names of many and many a captive who fretted his life away here, and left no record of himself but these sad epitaphs wrought with his own hands. They could not bear the thought of being utterly forgotten by the world.

MARK TWAIN, *The Innocents Abroad,* 1870

Saint Tropez

S. Tropez, charming little town as it is, is nevertheless not a place that can ever become a winter residence, as it looks to the north and is lashed by the terrible Mistral. But it has the advantage denied to the other towns on the coast, that, having the sun at the back, one looks from it upon the sea in all its intensity of colour without being dazzled. The town is divided into two parts—the old town and the new—and the former teems with picturesque features that attract the artist.

S. BARING-GOULD, *A Book of the Riviera*, 1905

Valley near Oloron-Ste.-Marie

There are little green hills alternating with green hollows, with a delightful absence of regularity, full of caprice and imagination. The meadows, constantly freshened by mists and rain, are framed with hedges of oak. Rain, or the weeping of the mist, forever descends upon the green oak summits. Verdure succeeds to verdure, and in their uniformity of fresh life, half-smiling and half-sad, there is a pleasing casualness, a quaint diversity of outline, caused by the uneven soil and the patterns of the fields.

H. A. TAINE, *Journeys Through France*, 1865

Cork Forest in the Maures

The forms of the Montagnes des Maures are rounded, and there are no bold crags; but it is scooped out into valleys that descend rapidly to the sea and to little bays; and these scoopings afford shelter from winter winds and cold, facing the sun, and walled in from every blast. Now the southern face of the Maures is precisely such a snuggery formed by Nature. The mountains curve about to focus the sun's rays; and the cork wood, evergreen, kill all glare. Here the date trees ripen their fruit; here the icy blasts do not shrivel up the eucalyptus, and smite down the oranges. The mountains are mantled in cork wood, save the bald heads of some, and the making of corks is the main industry of the scattered villages. Beside the manufacture of corks, the inhabitants of the Maures breed silkworms, and so grow mulberry trees for their sustenance.

S. BARING-GOULD, *A Book of the Riviera,* 1905

The Great Rose Window at Rheims

The rose window was not Gothic but Romanesque, and needed a great deal of coaxing to feel at home within the pointed arch. At first, the architects felt the awkwardness so strongly that they avoided it wherever they could. Rheims boldly imprisoned the roses within the pointed arch. In the beautiful facade of Laon, one of the chief beauties is the setting of the rose under a deep round arch. The western roses of Mantes and Paris are treated in the same way, although a captious critic might complain that their treatment is not so effective or so logical.

HENRY ADAMS, *Mont-Saint-Michel and Chartres*, 1905

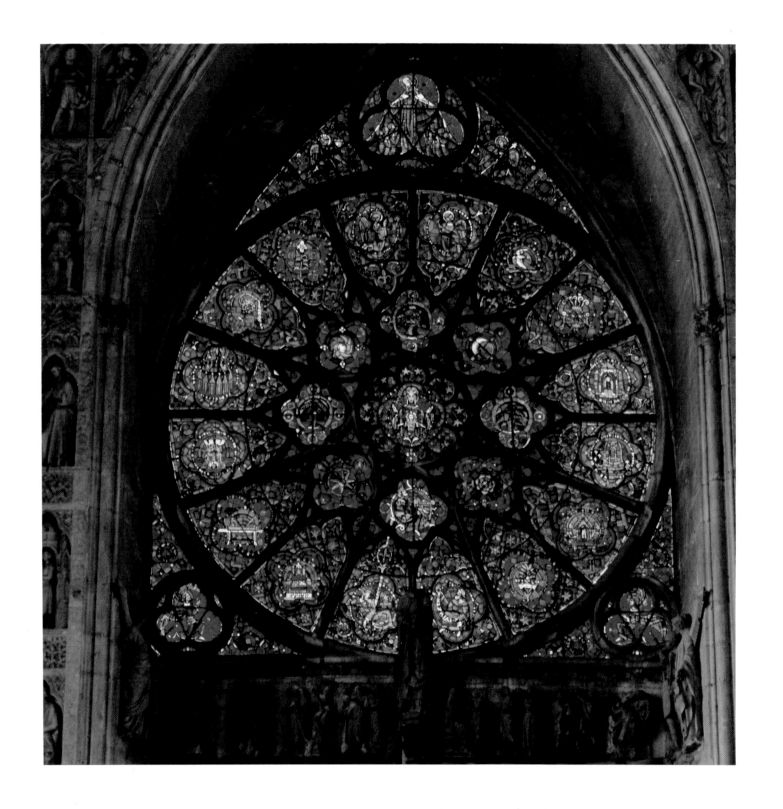

Domremy, Birthplace of St. Joan of Arc

Of Saint Joan: She was sixteen now, shapely and graceful, and of a beauty so extraordinary that I might allow myself any extravagance of language in describing it and yet have no fear of going beyond the truth. There was in her face a sweetness and serenity and purity that justly reflected her spiritual nature. She was deeply religious, and this is a thing which sometimes gives a melancholy cast to a person's countenance, but it was not so in her case. Her religion made her inwardly content and joyous; and if she was troubled at times, and showed the pain of it in her face and bearing, it came of distress for her country; no part of it was chargeable to her religion.

(From the writing of The Sieur Louis de Conte, her page and secretary, freely translated out of the ancient French into modern English from the original unpublished manuscript in the National Archives of France.)

MARK TWAIN, *Recollections of Joan of Arc,* 1896

Foothills of the Cevennes

The sky adds to the pleasantness and cheerfulness of the country. The velvet southern sky begins at this point, a radiant blue infused with light, like the clearest crystal. This lovely colour, sparkling and tender, sheds a glow of happiness over the trees, over the long stretch of fertile fields; the whole landscape resembles a garden, not the formal, plotted, economised garden of England, but somewhat casually tended, with a suggestion of neglect, though man's light-hearted negligence robs him of no whit of earth's prodigality.

H. A. TAINE, *Journeys Through France*, 1865

Saverne, Ancient Border Town

Fresh water always puts new life into me, especially when it flows full between its banks, and is green, and ripples with little waves. The glazed walls, the pretty houses, capriciously and irregularly built, glimmer in the water; set off by the intense green of the occasional poplars, steeped in the humid atmosphere, and girt around by the floating mist —a shifting veil of fog, banks of cloud and tattered bands of vapour, which rolls by or condenses as it falls.

H. A. TAINE, *Journeys Through France,* 1865

In the Valley of the Oise

It was the last good hour of the day. On the other
side of the valley a belfry showed among the foliage.
Thence some inspired bell-ringer made the afternoon
musical on a chime of bells. At last the bells ceased,
and with their note the sun withdrew. The piece was
at an end; shadow and silence possessed the valley
of the Oise.

ROBERT LOUIS STEVENSON, *An Inland Voyage,* 1879

A Word from the Photographer

My wife and I flew over the beautiful fields of Normandy for the first time in 1960. As we lowered for our landing at Orly, little French roads came into focus, and finally farm buildings, neat, green, golden, and red in the early morning sun. We stepped into another world. My childhood study of French at my grandmother's insistence; our schoolhouse and French teachers; Dumas, D'Artagnan, Daudet; picture books of Joan of Arc, Guynemer, and Marshall Foch; my war experiences in Algeria; all of these and more crowded about us as we left the plane. Well, that was the beginning. Later we sought scholarly material which would give us a better understanding. The effort in this collection is to bring you photographic material of subjects in rural France and some literary expressions and insights which we hope will give pleasure. My cameras are Hasselblad; lenses are Zeiss; film, Eastman CPS negative and its successors. The master prints were laser-scanned to provide high-quality page reproductions. It's said that it is impossible to teach a photographer to see, for this is a gift; but his seeing can be fine tuned. Minor White, my master teacher later in my experience, accomplished this for me. I want to communicate the excitement of the beauty so easily found everywhere in the French countryside. I hope the message is clear; that memories are stirred; that imaginations are heightened.

Proctor Jones

Shepherd near Albi

Acknowledgements

For patience, help, and understanding: my wife, Martha; our sons, Beverly and Proctor Jr.; our daughters, Martha and Jessica; and our friend, Mary Piel; all of whom drove, carried, scouted, and otherwise kept me company. William Walsh Mulvey gave early and valuable counsel to me.

For their comment and encouragement: Ambassador Claude Batault; Chief of Protocol Emmanuel de Casteja; Gerald Van der Kemp, Member of the Institute, former Inspector General of the Museums of France, and retired Chief Conservator of the Museum of Versailles and the Trianon, and Mrs. Van der Kemp; Dr. Charles Wiles; Jean Jose Clement, Deputy to the European Parliament; Pierre Lemoine, Conservator in Chief of the Chateau of Versailles; Annie Duprée, French Information Service, Quai d'Orsay, who helped to get the project started; Claire Joyce Toulgouat for her assistance at Giverny. The French Consulate General at San Francisco has provided effective cooperation: Consuls General Pierre de Mirmont, Pierre Brochand, and Gerard Errera; and Deputy Consul General Olivier Poupard. Estelle Barrett assisted greatly in the choice of photographs and language.

For dedication and service beyond the call of duty: my secretaries, Esta Swig and Victoria Carlyle. Candace Naploha provided the editing.

And finally, for competent and cheerful professional assistance: George Waters; Joyce and Adrian Wilson; Maria Therese Caen; and the Faulkner Color Lab, especially Tanya Lewis and Linda Stalter.

We are grateful to all who have been kind enough to help us in this work.

The Belvedere at the Petit Trianon, Versailles

Index

Designed by Adrian Wilson

Text set by Mackenzie-Harris Corp. in Centaur and Arrighi.
Display type set at The Press in Tuscany Alley in Michelangelo,
Palatino, and Palatino Italic

Laser scanned color separations and photolithography executed
by Pacific Lithograph Company, San Francisco, under the
supervision of George Waters

Binding by Roswell Bindery, Phoenix

ISBN: 0-9608860-0-1 Hardbound
0-9608860-1-x Paperbound
Library of Congress Catalogue Card Number: 82-090191

Proctor Jones Publishing Co.
3760 Washington Street
San Francisco, CA 94118